LONELINESS
Uaigneas

By Gabriel Rosenstock

Gabriel Rosenstock
Haiku for older children
with a gallery of international art, old and new

Cover: Mykola Koidan

Published by the author, 2025.
Layout and design: Mandy Marcus

Haiku poems in response to artwork in Public Domain, or in Fair Use category, i.e. artwork that is widely available on the internet on such platforms as Artvee and Wikiart.

Ealaíontóirí / Artists

Ernst Henseler (An Ghearmáin / *Germany*)
....08

Ohara Koson (An tSeapáin / *Japan*)
....10

Zemlyakova Liudmila (An Bhéalarúis / *Belarus*)
....12

Padraig McCaul (Éire / *Ireland*)
....14

Anita Zotkina (SAM / *USA*)
....16

Ayelet Lalor (Éire / *Ireland*)
....18

Mykola Koidan (Úcráin/an Phortaingéil / *Ukraine/ Portugal*)
....20

George Fuller (SAM / *USA*)
....22

Childe Hassam (SAM / *USA*) 24

Ferdinand Hodler (An Eilvéis / *Switzerland*) 26

Marina Dieul (An Fhrainc/Ceanada / *France/Canada*) 28

Jean-Léon Gérôme (An Fhrainc / *France*) 30

Asai Chū (An tSeapáin / *Japan*) 32

Frederick Carl Frieseke (An Ghearmáin/SAM / *Germany/USA*) 34

Pierre-Auguste Renoir (An Fhrainc / *France*) 36

James Ensor (An Bheilg / *Belgium*) 38

Félix Ziem (An Fhrainc / *France*)
....40

Henry Inman (SAM / *USA*)
....42

Maruyama Okyo (An tSeapáin / *Japan*)
....44

Robert Henri (SAM / *USA*)
....46

Gustave Van de Woestyne (An Bheilg / *Belgium*)
....48

Emil Rudolf Weiss (An Ghearmáin / *Germany*)
....50

Daniel Koechlin (An Fhrainc / *France*)
....52

Gabriel von Max (An Ostair / *Austria*)
....54

Robert Caldwell (SAM / *USA*) 56

Norman Garstin (Éire / *Ireland*) 58

Benjamin Waterhouse Hawkins (An Bhreatain / *Britain*) 60

Abbott Handerson Thayer (SAM / *USA*) 62

Eliseo Meifrén (An Chatalóin / *Catalonia*) 64

Kazimierz Stabrowski (An Pholainn / *Poland*) 66

August Malmström (An tSualainn / *Sweden*) 68

Getsuju (An tSeapáin / *Japan*) 70

Karel Špillar (Poblacht na Seice / *Czech Republic*)
....72

Bruno Liljefors (An tSualainn / *Sweden*)
....74

Akseli Gallen-Kallela (An Fhionlainn / *Finland*)
....76

grág! grág!
frog i bhfolach
(dhá cheann b'fhéidir?)

croak! croak!
a frog hiding
(maybe two?)

faoileáin
tá rud éigin
ar a n-intinn acu

seagulls
they have something
on their mind

thaibhríos faoi dhuilleoga
ag titim – dhúisíos
bhí na duilleoga tite

I dreamed of falling leaves
and awoke – the leaves
had fallen

cad as ar tháinig siad
cá bhfuil a dtriall?
caoirigh ar an mbóthar

where did they come from
where are they going?
sheep on the road

tá tusa beo – táimse beo
tá na réaltaí beo
beathach beo, beo – ó!

you're alive – I'm alive
stars are alive
alive alive oh!

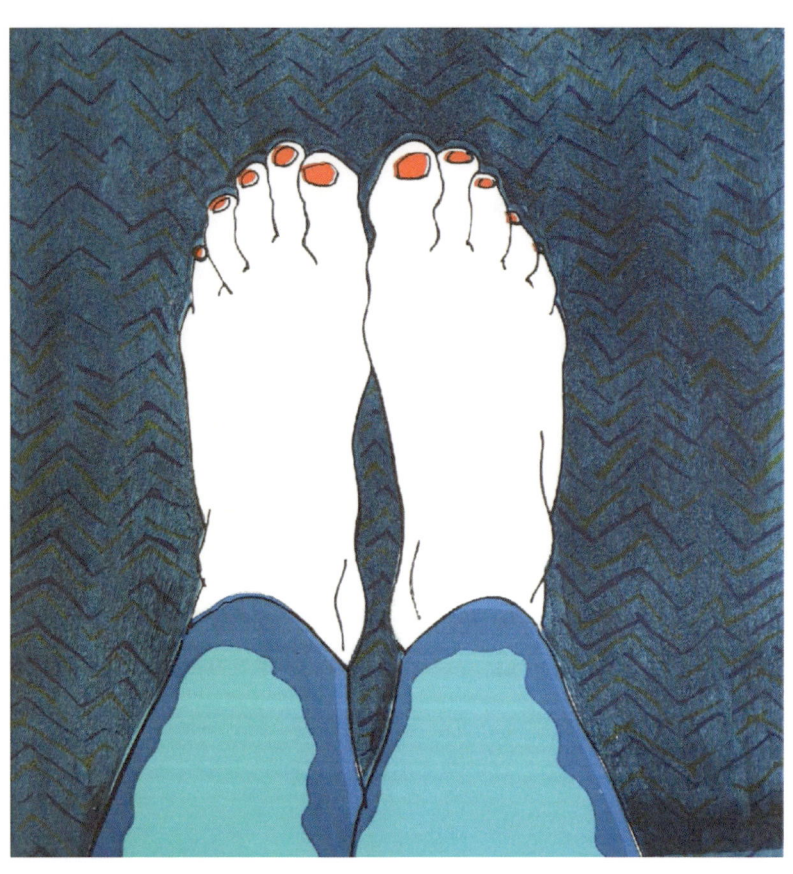

ingne coise mo dheirféar
go hachomair . . .
scanrúil

    my sister's toenails
    in a word . . .
    scary

uaigngeas   uagnuss
uignós . . .
nílim in ann é a litriú

lonilynes   loneyless
loynyliness . . .
I can't spell it

turcaithe á gcomhaireamh . . .
mearbhall ar chailín
na dturcaithe

counting turkeys . . .
the turkey-girl's head
is swimming

ceo . . .
capall is carráiste
ag teacht amach as ré eile

fog . . .
a horse and carriage emerge
from another century

gréasaí . . .
poll mór
ina bhróg

cobbler . . .
a large hole
in his shoe

a choinín bhig!
níl d'fhéasóga ar crith
níos mó

little rabbit!
your whiskers
have stopped trembling

" . . . is ansin na Briotanaigh –
san Ind!"
go n-éirí leat, a Bhónaí

" . . . and then I'll thrash the Brits –
in India!"
good luck, Napoleon

froganna
    foinse na gcuilithíní
    á lorg acu

frogs
    searching for the source
    of ripples

garsún óg . . .
a bhróga ag teacht
lena chuid gruaige

young boy . . .
shoes matching
his hair

ag léim amach
ón leathanach!
haiku mar gheall ar fhrog

*jumping
out of the page!
a haiku about a frog*

díoscán na rámhaí . . .
is annamh a chloiseann sé anois é
bádóir

creak of oars . . .
he rarely hears it now
boatman

cén teanga
a labhraíonn siad?
maighdeana mara

*what language
do they speak?
mermaids*

ní den ghramaisc é
sé No-Tin é – Gaoth –
Taoiseach

he's no Tom, Dick or Harry
No-Tin is he – Wind –
a Chief

siúil go séimh séimh . . .
ár gcruinne
leochaileach

tread softly, softly . . .
our fragile
universe

cad is féidir liom á rá?
faic! faic in aon chor . . .
tá píopa im' ghob

what can I say?
nothing! nothing at all . . .
I've a pipe in my mouth

d'fhéadfaidís teacht ina gcuileoga
cá bhfios . . .
eachtardhomhandaigh

    they could come disguised as flies
    you never know . . .
    extraterrestrials

fear grinn ab ea a athair . . .
agus a athair siúd
chomh maith

his father was a clown . . .
and his father's father
as well

yûgure a oya nashi suzume nanto naku*

    clapsholas –
    gealbhan gan mháthair
    ag caoineadh

        twilight –
        a motherless sparrow
        crying

*Haiku by Issa, 1810

haiku Issa
faoin ngealbhan bocht gan
mháthair . . . an-bhrónach!

Issa's haiku
about a poor motherless
sparrow . . . sad!

coiligh . . .
i mbun mioscaise?
deacair a rá

    roosters . . .
    up to some mischief?
    hard to say

i bhfolach
(chualadar an bháisteach ag teacht)
seangáin is feithidí

in hiding
(they heard the rain coming)
ants and insects

á!
aer na farraige . . .
spreagann sé an goile

ah!
sea air . . .
gives you an appetite

an bhfuil tú ansin
heileo, a fhroig –
an tú atá ann?

are you there
hello, frog –
is that you?

báid fholmha
á líonadh
le ciúnas

empty boats
filling up
with silence

préacháin
ní i mbun comhdhála iad
gan chúis

crows
they've come together
for some purpose

ní ghéilleann an chuid is mó díobh
do dhaoine . . .
an t-aos sí

most of them
don't believe in humans . . .
fairies

a fhroig!
cad atá ort?
cén fáth nach bpreabann tú?

frog!
what's wrong?
why don't you jump?

saoirse
na sairdíní
sula gcuirtear i gcannaí iad

*the freedom
of sardines
before they are canned*

feictear
ní fheictear é
an giorria sneachta

visible
invisible
the snow hare

garsún beag
préachán –
iad araon cosnochta

little boy
crow –
both barefoot

Iarfhocal / Afterword

What are you holding in your hand? A book of haiku and senryū. (A senryū looks like a haiku but it usually deals with people and is a lighter, more amusing form of haiku).

~

Haiku deal with those magical, mysterious moments we have with nature – clouds, trees, lakes, birds, the moon, flowers, frogs, the wind etc., everything in nature, throughout the seasons.

~

The haiku poet disappears, for a moment, in the thing described – the sound of a cuckoo, for instance, a rare sound now as various species disappear.

~

How sad it is when things vanish from the face of the earth – even a scent, or a sound. How tragic when a language dies! Are we doing enough to preserve the biodiversity of the world and its rich fabric of cultural diversity?

~

With haiku, we can awaken to an appreciation of the gift of awareness, awareness of beauty, awareness of life. Without this awakening, we miss out on the pulse of life. Instead of living life to the full, we get bored, or cynical!

~

What are ekphrastic haiku? Ekphrastic haiku are written in response to works of art, such as a painting or a sculpture.
Ekphrastic haiku sharpen our awareness of art and the beautiful mystery that is creativity itself.

~

There are many different forms of art, many different styles. Haiku, too, is an art. It looks simple, but only by reading – and writing haiku – do we acquire the knack.

~

Do you have a favourite haiku, or a work of art that you particularly like in this book, or in other books you have read? Why not keep a little diary? Transcribe the haiku you like and say why you like it.

~

The title of this book is *Uaigneas/Loneliness*. We can look at everything as a gift, even loneliness. In our loneliness we can open a book and read; we can contemplate; we can open up our hearts and our minds – then we're no longer lonely. Anything can become our companion, our haiku companion: a cloud, a worm, a drop of rain.

~

Pick a haiku that you like, from this book or any other collection of haiku you find, and make a postcard, a birthday card, or an anniversary card for someone. Or celebrate some traditional festival with a card – maybe even a forgotten festival no longer remembered today!

~

If you have a second language, translate a haiku into that language. It need not be on paper. You could create a haiku artefact with wood, or use chalk, crayons, or even paint on a rock, or stone. It could be a representation of the subject matter of the haiku in a realist or in an abstract style. Your choice.

Happy haiku days!

Gabriel Rosenstock
Baile Átha Cliath (Dublin)
Éire (Ireland)

Gabriel Rosenstock in Smock Alley Theatre, Dublin, on Thursday, 17 November, 2022 where Gabriel adjudicated **Duais Bashō** and presented awards to prize winners.

Duais Bashō (The Bashō Prize) is a joint venture between IMRAM, the Irish-language literature festival, and Poetry Ireland, the national poetry organisation. This annual competition is open to bilingual haiku from schoolchildren on the island of Ireland.

Further Reading

Fluttering their way into my head:
An exploration of haiku for young people
(Evertype, *2014*)

Sneachta: *transcreations in Irish & English of Issa's snow haiku*
(The Onslaught Press, *2016*)

Haiku, más é do thoil é!
Irish-language book for young readers, exploring the joy of haiku
(An Gúm, *2014*)

A Sweater for the Tayfel:
Bilingual haiku in response to artwork by Issacher Ber Rybek (Ukraine)
(Buttonhook Press, *2022*)

Meditation on Known Mysteries
Tanka poems in Irish and English, 31 syllables in a configuration of 5-7-5-7-7
(Published by the author, *2025*)

www.ingramcontent.com/pod-product-compliance
Lightning Source LLC
Chambersburg PA
CBRC090749020526
44118CB00030B/251